The God Really Loves You Book Series™ Presents:

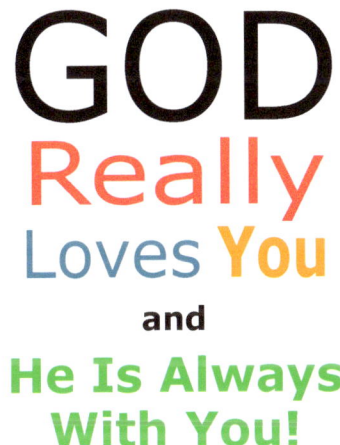

GOD Really Loves You
and
He Is Always With You!

**Written and Illustrated
by Wendy Nelson**

God Really Loves You Book Series™ presents:

GOD Really Loves You
and He Is Always With You!

Text Copyright ©2019 by Wendy Nelson
Artwork Copyright ©2019 by Wendy Nelson

Published by MediaTek Grafx
POB 62, Bonnieville, Kentucky, 42713

ISBN 978-0-578-52228-9

Design and production by MediaTek Grafx, Bonnieville, Kentucky.

The Publisher has made every effort to avoid errors or omissions. Opinions, stories, and themes are intended for entertainment, motivation for research and future study. This book includes content that is non-fiction.

All Scripture quotations are from the The Holy Bible, King James Version, Pradis Software Rel 02.04.03, Built with Conform Version 5.00.0051, Version 5.1.50 Copyright ©2002 The Zondervan Corporation All Rights Reserved.

All rights reserved. This Publication may not be reproduced in whole or in part, stored or transmitted by any means. Media may use small portions for reviews. Please request written permission from Publisher for any other reason.

Printed in the United States of America

A Special Gift for

―――――――――――

From

―――――――――――

Note

―――――――――――――――――
―――――――――――――――――
―――――――――――――――――

Date

―――――――――――

God is our Father in Heaven
and He is always with us!

1 John 4:4 Ye are of God, little children, and have overcome them: because greater is he that is in you, than he that is in the world.

You are special,
and God loves you very much!

This much
is a whole bunch!

God really loves everyone!

*Proverbs 8:17 I love them that love me;
and those that seek me early shall find me.*

He is with you
when you are sad!

God is with you when you feel lonely.

John 14:16-17 And I will pray the Father, and he shall give you another Comforter, that he may abide with you for ever; Even the Spirit of truth; whom the world cannot receive, because it seeth him not, neither knoweth him: but ye know him; for he dwelleth with you, and shall be in you.

When you have trouble,
God is with you.

Look for nice things around you,
instead of being angry.

Deuteronomy 20:4 For the Lord your God is he that goeth with you, to fight for you against your enemies, to save you.

Are you afraid, sometimes?
Smile and know
that God is with you!

He helps you be brave
in loud, booming
thunder storms!

*Isaiah 41:10 Fear thou not; for I am with thee:
be not dismayed; for I am thy God:
I will strengthen thee;
yea, I will help thee; yea, I will uphold thee
with the right hand of my righteousness.*

You make God happy!
He rejoices over you!

Zephaniah 3:17 The Lord thy God in the midst of thee is mighty; he will save, he will rejoice over thee with joy; he will rest in his love, he will joy over thee with singing.

Do you need help?
God is a helper.

Mommy and daddy are helpers.

Sisters and brothers are helpers.

*Psalms 54:4 Behold, God is mine helper:
the Lord is with them that uphold my soul.*

In your heart,
is where God is!

You have
a happy
heart!

John 14:27 Peace I leave with you, my peace I give unto you: not as the world giveth, give I unto you. Let not your heart be troubled, neither let it be afraid.

Whatever you are doing,
God is there!

He is with you when you are running, working, reading, building with blocks, sleeping or drawing!

Genesis 21:22 And it came to pass at that time, that Abimelech and Phichol the chief captain of his host spake unto Abraham, saying,
God is with thee in all that thou doest:

Love God
with all of your heart!

Matthew 22:37-38 Jesus said unto him, Thou shalt love the Lord thy God with all thy heart, and with all thy soul, and with all thy mind.
This is the first and great commandment.

God is with you when you are learning to bake.

God is with you when you are learning to build.

1 Corinthians 3:16 Know ye not that ye are the temple of God, and that the Spirit of God dwelleth in you?

Nobody can take
God away from you.

God
is always
with you.

Romans 8:39 Nor height, nor depth, nor any other creature, shall be able to separate us from the love of God, which is in Christ Jesus our Lord.

Learn about God.
God loves you
and He is always with you!

Ephesians 5:1 Be ye therefore followers of God, as dear children;

God Really Loves You Book Series™

GodReallyLovesYou.com

2 Thessalonians 3:5 And the Lord direct your hearts into the love of God, and into the patient waiting for Christ.

Matthew 18:3-5 And said, Verily I say unto you, Except ye be converted, and become as little children, ye shall not enter into the kingdom of heaven. Whosoever therefore shall humble himself as this little child, the same is greatest in the kingdom of heaven. And whoso shall receive one such little child in my name receiveth me.

www.ingramcontent.com/pod-product-compliance
Lightning Source LLC
Chambersburg PA
CBHW041400160426
42811CB00101B/1488